TAKE IT APART
HELICOPTER

By Chris Oxlade

Illustrated by Mike Grey

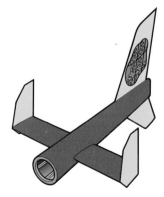

Silver Press
Parsippany, New Jersey

First published in the U.K. in 1996 by

 Belitha Press Limited, London House,
Great Eastern Wharf, Parkgate Road,
London SW11 4NQ

Printed in China

Editor: Jilly MacLeod
Designer: Guy Callaby
Illustrator: Mike Grey
Consultant: Lindsay Peacock

Published in the United States in 1997 by

 Silver Press
A Division of Simon & Schuster
299 Jefferson Road
Parsippany, New Jersey 07054

Library of Congress Cataloging-in-Publication Data
Oxlade, Chris
Helicopter/by Chris Oxlade.
p.   cm. (Take it apart!)
Originally published: London, England: Belitha Press Limited, 1996.
IIncludes index.
Summary: Describes the parts of a helicopter and how they work.
1. Helicopters–Parts–Juvenile literature. I. Series.
TL716.2.095   1997 96-26998
629.133'352–dc20 CIP AC
IISBN 0-382-39669-3 (LSB) 10 9 8 7 6 5 4 3 2 1
IISBN 0-382-39670-7 (PBK) 10 9 8 7 6 5 4 3 2 1

Inside This Book

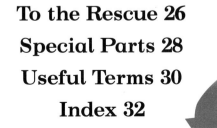

Take a Helicopter Apart

◉ A helicopter is made of thousands of different parts.

◉ The parts are made of metal, plastic, glass, and many other special materials.

◉ All the parts are put together in an aircraft factory.

◉ This book shows you the main parts of a passenger helicopter and how they fit together.

Fact Box
The first helicopter to lift a person into the air was built by a Frenchman named Paul Cornu in 1907.

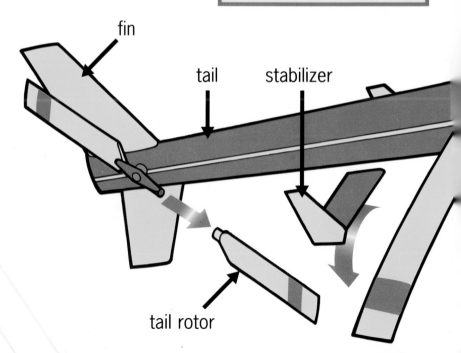

fin

tail

stabilizer

tail rotor

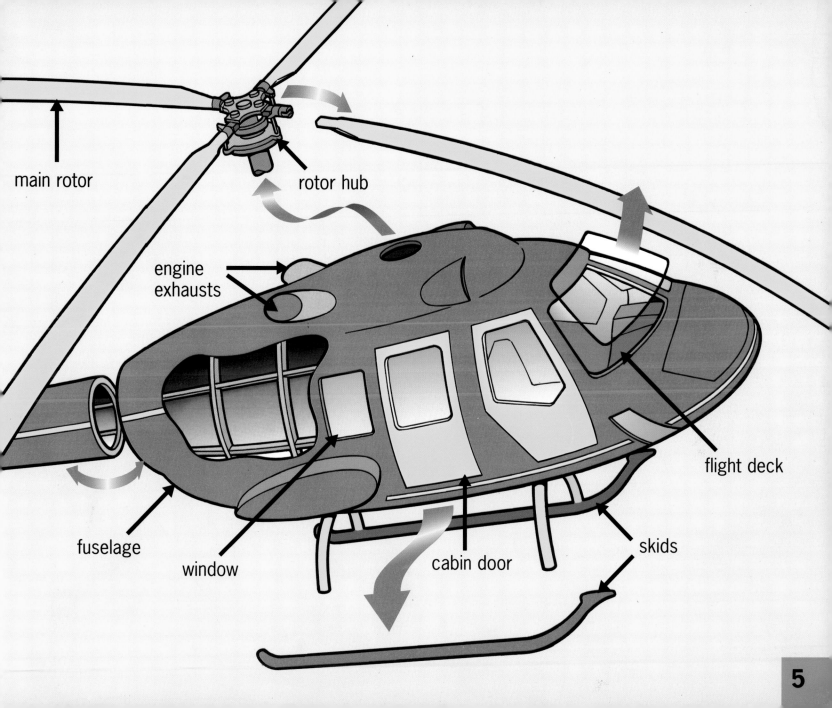

main rotor

rotor hub

engine
exhausts

flight deck

fuselage

window

cabin door

skids

The Fuselage

● The fuselage is the main part of the helicopter. This is where the passengers and the pilots sit.

● The fuselage is like a large metal box, with holes in the sides for windows and doors.

● All the other parts of the helicopter are attached to the fuselage.

● Inside the fuselage is a metal floor. The passengers' seats are fastened to the floor.

Fact Box
The largest helicopter ever built was the Russian Mil V-12. Its fuselage was 12 feet long –as long as a jet airliner.

The engine casing
A special casing on top of the fuselage houses the engines. There is a hole in the top of the casing for the rotor shaft to pass through (see page 8).

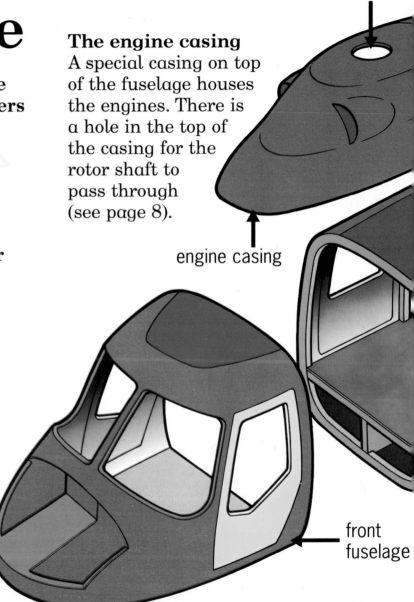

hole for rotor shaft

engine casing

front fuselage

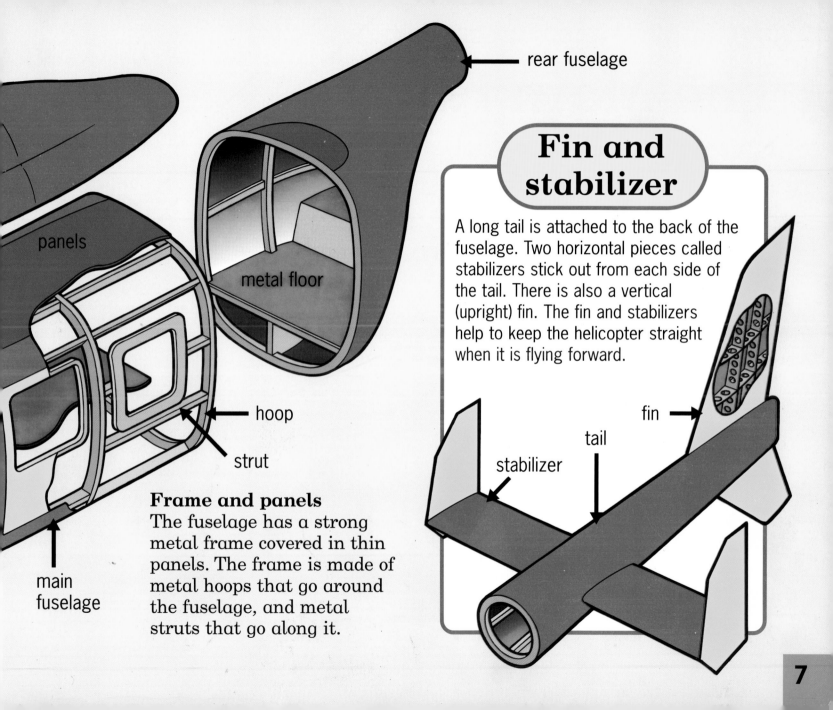

rear fuselage

panels

metal floor

hoop

strut

main fuselage

Frame and panels

The fuselage has a strong metal frame covered in thin panels. The frame is made of metal hoops that go around the fuselage, and metal struts that go along it.

Fin and stabilizer

A long tail is attached to the back of the fuselage. Two horizontal pieces called stabilizers stick out from each side of the tail. There is also a vertical (upright) fin. The fin and stabilizers help to keep the helicopter straight when it is flying forward.

fin

tail

stabilizer

The Main Rotor

● The main rotor lifts the helicopter into the air.

● The rotor has long, thin rotor blades that are fastened to a rotor hub.

● The rotor blades spin around very fast. As they spin, they push air downward and lift the helicopter into the air.

● The main rotor also pushes the helicopter forward, backward or sideways.

rotor spins
this way

rotor hub

shaft from
engine

Fact Box
Some large helicopters have two main rotors instead of one. The rotors may be mounted one above the other, or one at the front of the helicopter and one at the back.

glass-fiber skin

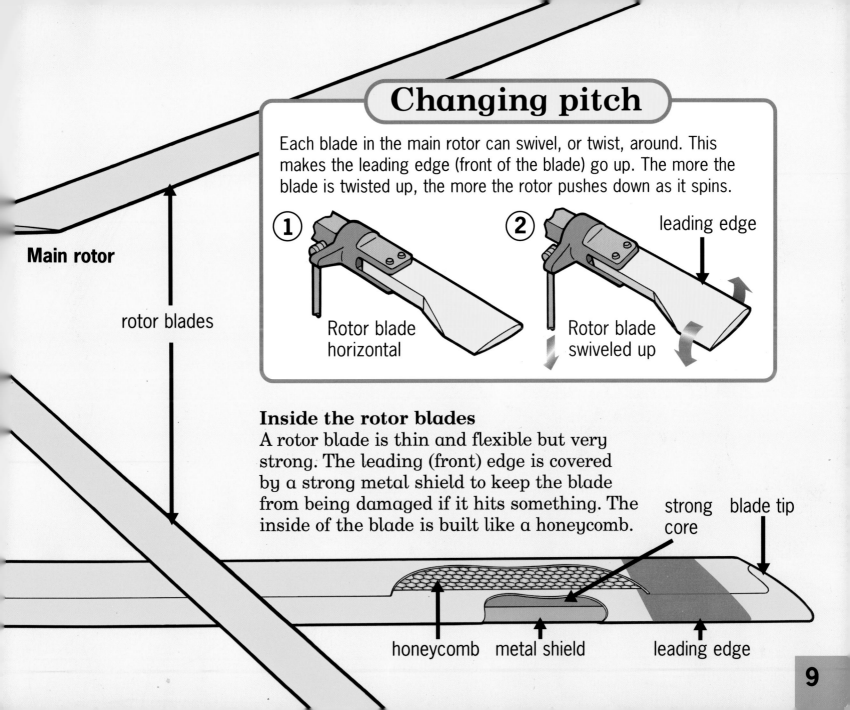

Main rotor

rotor blades

Changing pitch

Each blade in the main rotor can swivel, or twist, around. This makes the leading edge (front of the blade) go up. The more the blade is twisted up, the more the rotor pushes down as it spins.

① Rotor blade horizontal

② Rotor blade swiveled up

leading edge

Inside the rotor blades

A rotor blade is thin and flexible but very strong. The leading (front) edge is covered by a strong metal shield to keep the blade from being damaged if it hits something. The inside of the blade is built like a honeycomb.

strong core

blade tip

honeycomb   metal shield   leading edge

The Tail Rotor

- The tail rotor is at the back of the helicopter, out of the way of the main rotor.

- The tail rotor has blades, just like the main rotor.

- Without a tail rotor, the fuselage would spin around in the opposite direction to the main rotor.

- The tail rotor helps the helicopter to turn left or right.

Fact Box
On helicopters with two main rotors, one rotor spins in one direction, and the other spins the opposite way. This means the helicopter does not need a tail rotor.

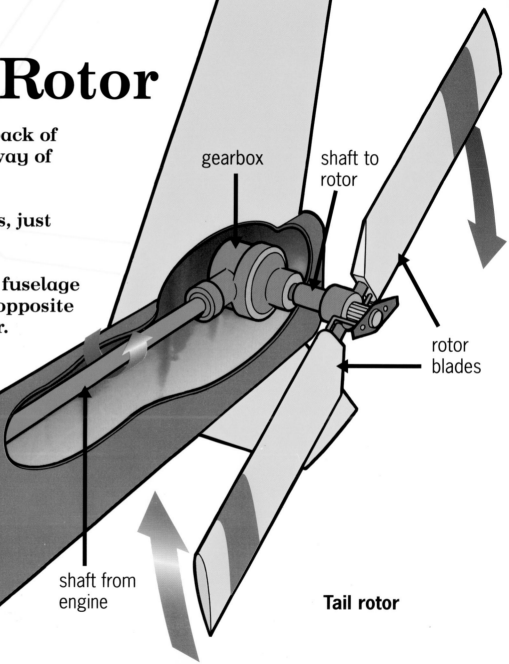

gearbox

shaft to rotor

rotor blades

shaft from engine

Tail rotor

What the tail rotor does

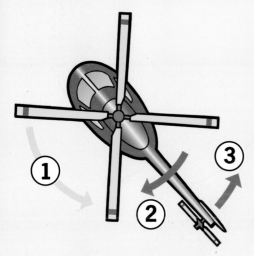

① ③ ②

1 The main rotor spins around to lift the helicopter into the air.

2 As the main rotor spins in one direction, the fuselage tries to spin in the opposite direction.

3 The tail rotor tries to push the tail around in the same direction as the main rotor. This cancels the spinning effect of the fuselage and keeps the helicopter steady.

Gears in the tail

When the engine is running, it turns a shaft that makes the tail rotor go around. But because the rotor is on the side of the tail –at right angles to the shaft–gears are used to turn the corner. You can find out more about gears on page 14.

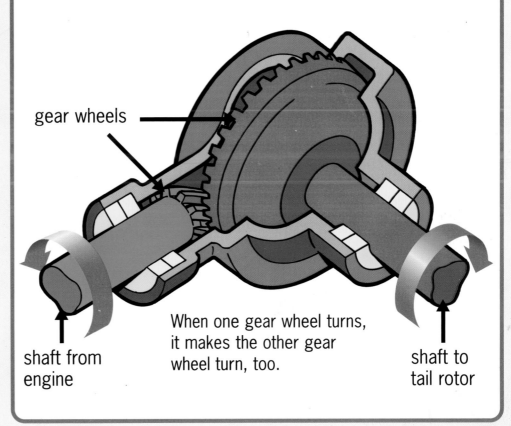

gear wheels

When one gear wheel turns, it makes the other gear wheel turn, too.

shaft from engine

shaft to tail rotor

The Engines

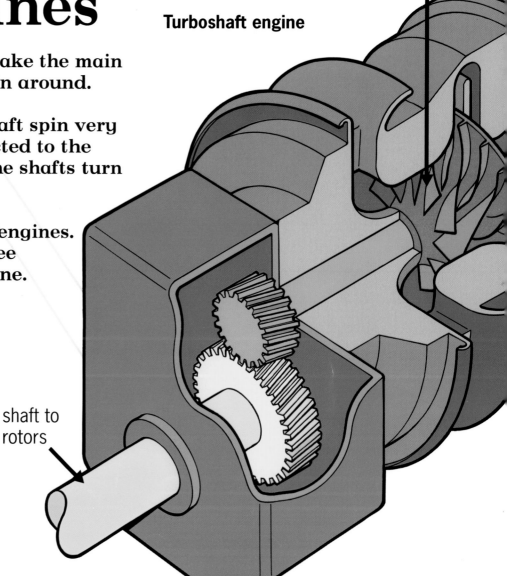

Turboshaft engine

compressor

⊘ A helicopter's engines make the main rotor and the tail rotor spin around.

⊘ Each engine makes a shaft spin very fast. The shafts are connected to the rotors, and as they spin, the shafts turn the rotors around.

⊘ This helicopter has two engines. Some helicopters have three engines; others have just one.

⊘ The engines are called turboshafts.

shaft to rotors

Fact Box
Even if all its engines break down, a helicopter can still glide safely to the ground.

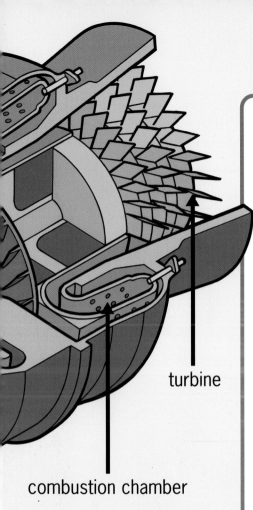

turbine

combustion chamber

How the engine works

1 Compressor

Inside the engine there is a part called a compressor. It has spinning fans that suck in air and squeeze it into the combustion chamber.

air in

shaft to rotors

hot gases out

2 Combustion chamber

Inside the combustion chamber the air is used to burn fuel. As the fuel burns, it makes a stream of hot gases.

3 Turbine

The hot gases shoot through a part called a turbine, making it spin very fast. As it spins, the turbine makes the shaft to the rotors spin as well. It also spins the compressor.

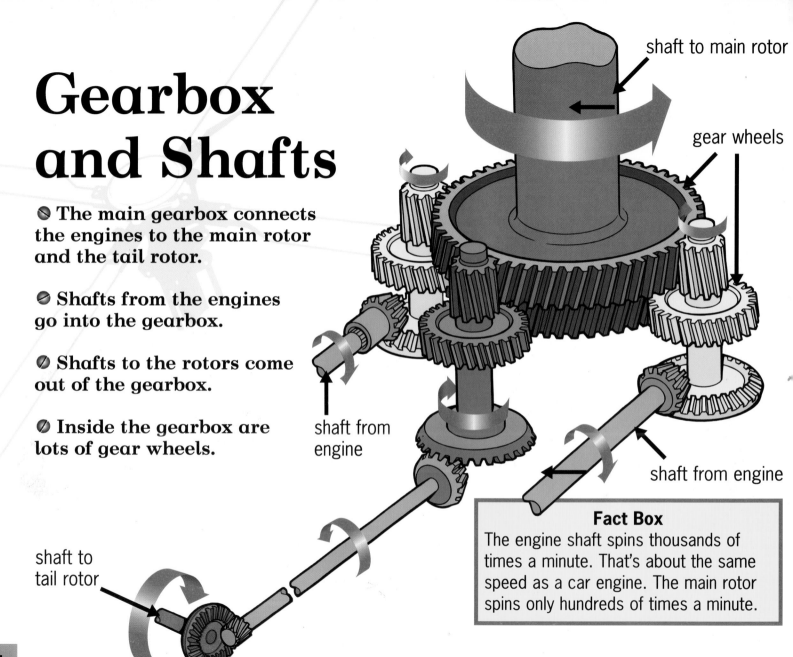

Gearbox and Shafts

⚙ The main gearbox connects the engines to the main rotor and the tail rotor.

⚙ Shafts from the engines go into the gearbox.

⚙ Shafts to the rotors come out of the gearbox.

⚙ Inside the gearbox are lots of gear wheels.

shaft to main rotor

gear wheels

shaft from engine

shaft from engine

shaft to tail rotor

Fact Box
The engine shaft spins thousands of times a minute. That's about the same speed as a car engine. The main rotor spins only hundreds of times a minute.

teeth

Gear wheels
The gear wheels have teeth around them that lock together with the teeth in other gear wheels. When one wheel turns, it makes the other wheel turn.

The gearbox also has shafts that go to electrical generators. When the shafts in the generators spin, they make electricity for the helicopter's navigation equipment, flight controls, and cabin lights.

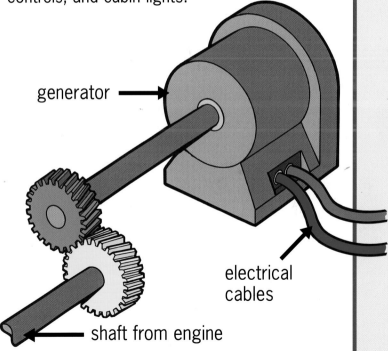

generator

electrical cables

shaft from engine

The Skids

⏺ **Some helicopters land on metal parts called skids.**

⏺ **The skids are attached to the fuselage frame by curved legs.**

⏺ **Most small helicopters have skids.**

⏺ **Larger helicopters have wheels like the landing gear on a plane.**

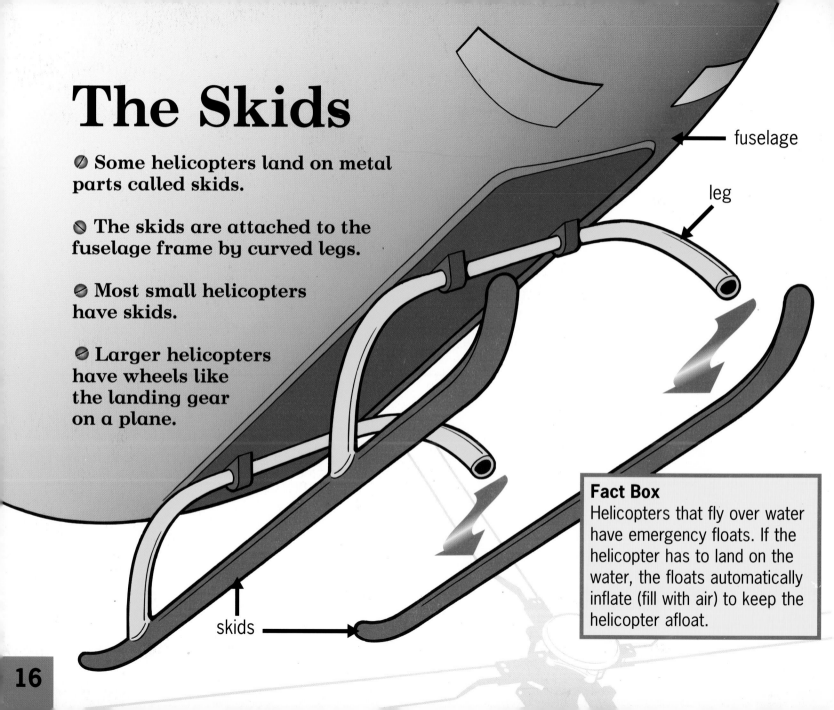

fuselage

leg

skids

Fact Box
Helicopters that fly over water have emergency floats. If the helicopter has to land on the water, the floats automatically inflate (fill with air) to keep the helicopter afloat.

Landing gear

Sets of wheels that let a helicopter move along the ground are called landing gear. The wheels are folded away after takeoff and lowered again before landing. The front wheels can be turned to steer the helicopter on the ground.

nose wheel

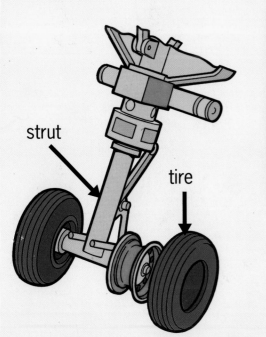

strut

tire

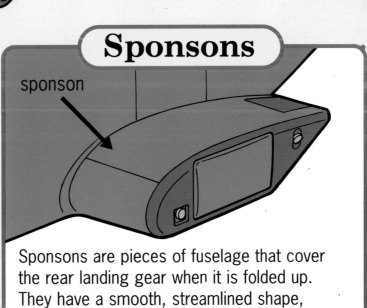

Sponsons

sponson

rear landing gear

Sponsons are pieces of fuselage that cover the rear landing gear when it is folded up. They have a smooth, streamlined shape, which helps the helicopter to go faster.

The Cockpit

● The cockpit is at the front of the helicopter. It is where the pilot and copilot sit.

● The cockpit contains all the controls and instruments the pilots need to fly the helicopter.

● Instruments in the cockpit give the pilots information about the helicopter, such as its speed, its altitude (height), and how much fuel is left.

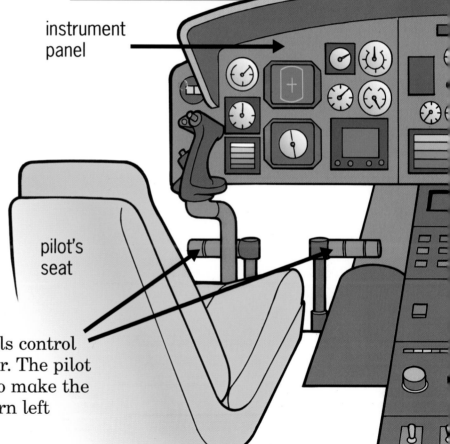

instrument panel

pilot's seat

Turning

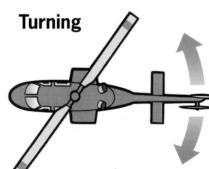

Foot pedals
The foot pedals control the tail rotor. The pilot uses them to make the helicopter turn left or right.

Collective pitch lever
The collective pitch lever changes the speed of the rotors and the angle of the main rotor blades. The pilot uses the lever to make the helicopter go up or down.

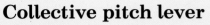

Up and down

Backward, forward, left, or right

Control column
The pilot uses the control column to make the helicopter move forward, backward, left, or right.

copilot's seat

Electronics

There are many miles of electrical wires in a helicopter. The computerized navigation equipment is kept in the nose near the pilots' feet.

Doors and Windows

● The pilots and passengers get into and out of the helicopter through doors in the side of the fuselage.

● This helicopter has two doors, which open on hinges.

● Larger helicopters have several doors. Some doors fold down to open; others slide open.

● The windows fit into holes in the fuselage. They let the pilots and passengers see out, and let light into the cabin and cockpit.

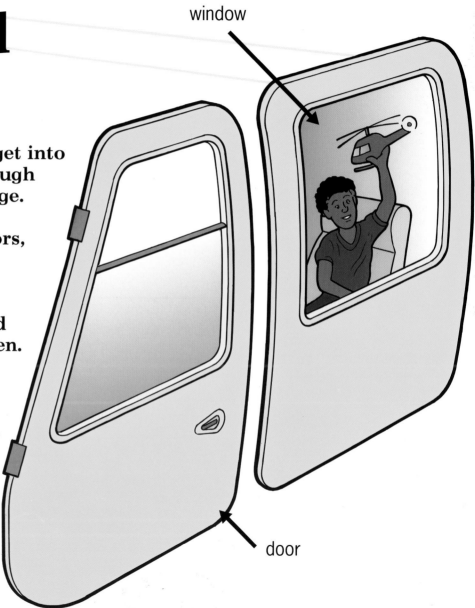

window

door

20

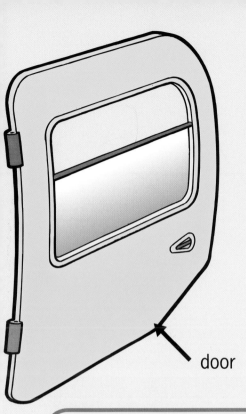

door

windshield wipers

Cockpit windows

Passenger steps

On some larger helicopters, one of the doors folds downward so that the top of the door touches the ground. On the back of the door is a set of steps for passengers to walk down.

Cockpit windows

The cockpit windows give pilots a good all-around view. There is a wide, fixed window in front of each pilot, and windows that open on each side. Small windows above the pilots' heads and by their feet let the pilots see the sky and the ground.

Inside the Cabin

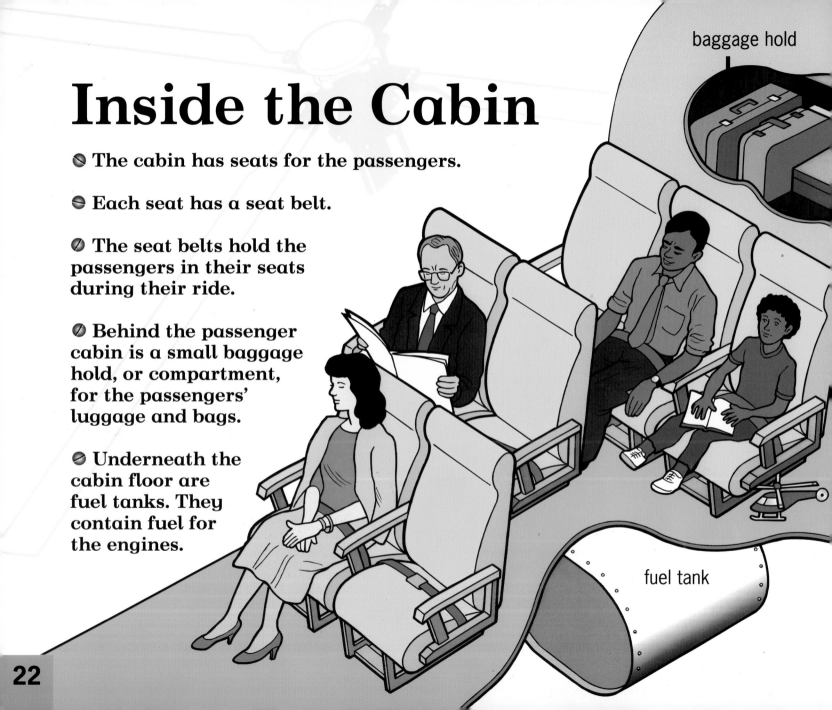

- The cabin has seats for the passengers.

- Each seat has a seat belt.

- The seat belts hold the passengers in their seats during their ride.

- Behind the passenger cabin is a small baggage hold, or compartment, for the passengers' luggage and bags.

- Underneath the cabin floor are fuel tanks. They contain fuel for the engines.

baggage hold

fuel tank

headrest

seat belt

armrest

Seats

The passengers' seats are firmly fastened to the floor with bolts. Each seat has a seat belt, headrest, and armrests.

Safety equipment

Helicopters that fly over water carry special safety equipment, such as exposure suits, life jackets, and life rafts. These help passengers and crew to survive if the helicopter has to crash-land in water.

exposure suit

life raft

life jacket

Building a Helicopter

⊘ Building helicopters takes lots of space, so they have to be built in large factories.

⊖ Different parts of the helicopter are made in different factories. Then they are taken to the factory where the helicopter is put together.

⊖ It takes months to build each helicopter.

The first stages
The fuselage is built first. Then all the electrical wires and instruments are put in.

Pulling in the engines
Next the engines, gears, and rotor hubs are added, along with the skids.

Finishing

The seats, doors, and windows are put in next. Finally, the rotor blades are added.

Flight testing

Every helicopter is tested in the air before it is delivered to the customer. Helicopters are very complicated, and testing takes many hours.

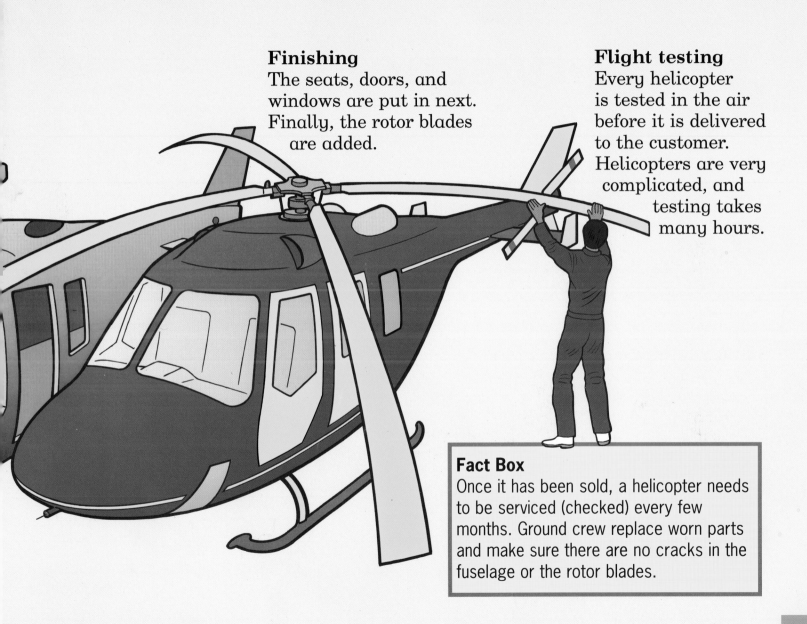

Fact Box

Once it has been sold, a helicopter needs to be serviced (checked) every few months. Ground crew replace worn parts and make sure there are no cracks in the fuselage or the rotor blades.

To the Rescue

- Some helicopters do special jobs.

- A rescue helicopter has special equipment so that it can search for and rescue people lost on water or on mountains.

- It can pick up injured or stranded people without landing.

- Rescue helicopters are often painted yellow to make them easy to see.

Stretchers
Inside the helicopter are stretchers for injured people to lie on. The stretchers can also be attached to the winch so that badly hurt people can be lifted up.

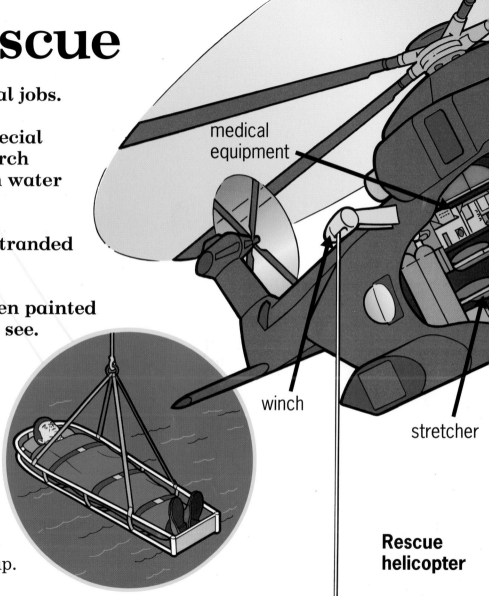

medical equipment

winch

stretcher

Rescue helicopter

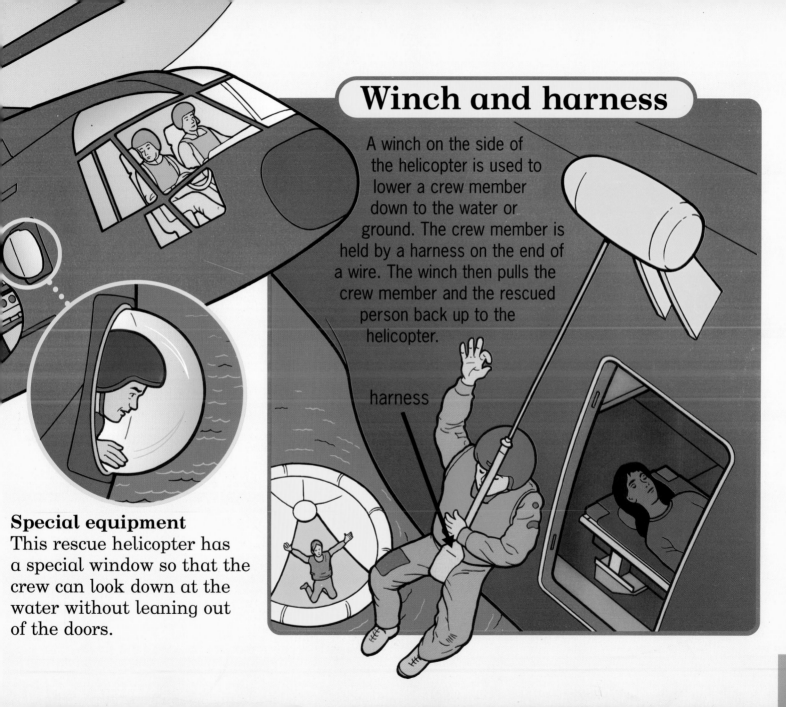

Winch and harness

A winch on the side of the helicopter is used to lower a crew member down to the water or ground. The crew member is held by a harness on the end of a wire. The winch then pulls the crew member and the rescued person back up to the helicopter.

harness

Special equipment
This rescue helicopter has a special window so that the crew can look down at the water without leaning out of the doors.

Special Parts

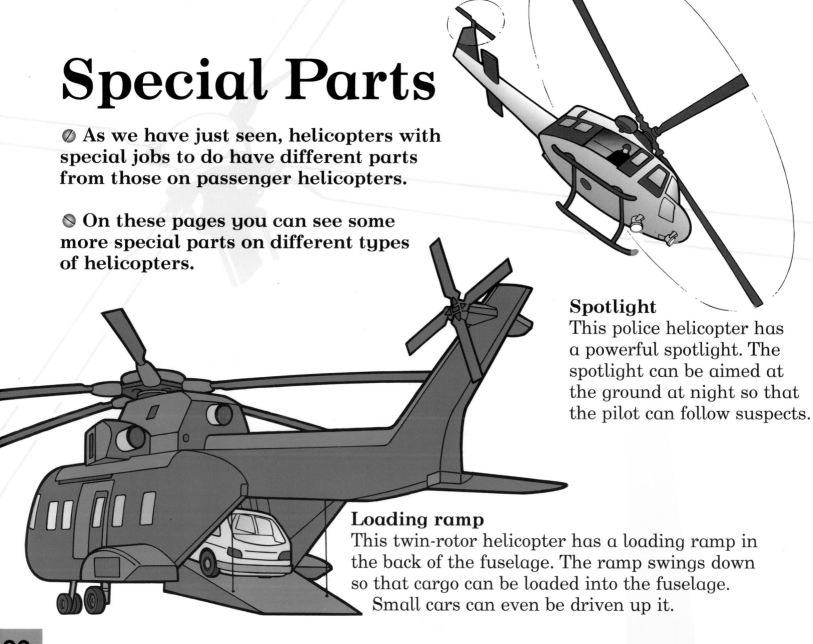

As we have just seen, helicopters with special jobs to do have different parts from those on passenger helicopters.

On these pages you can see some more special parts on different types of helicopters.

Spotlight
This police helicopter has a powerful spotlight. The spotlight can be aimed at the ground at night so that the pilot can follow suspects.

Loading ramp
This twin-rotor helicopter has a loading ramp in the back of the fuselage. The ramp swings down so that cargo can be loaded into the fuselage. Small cars can even be driven up it.

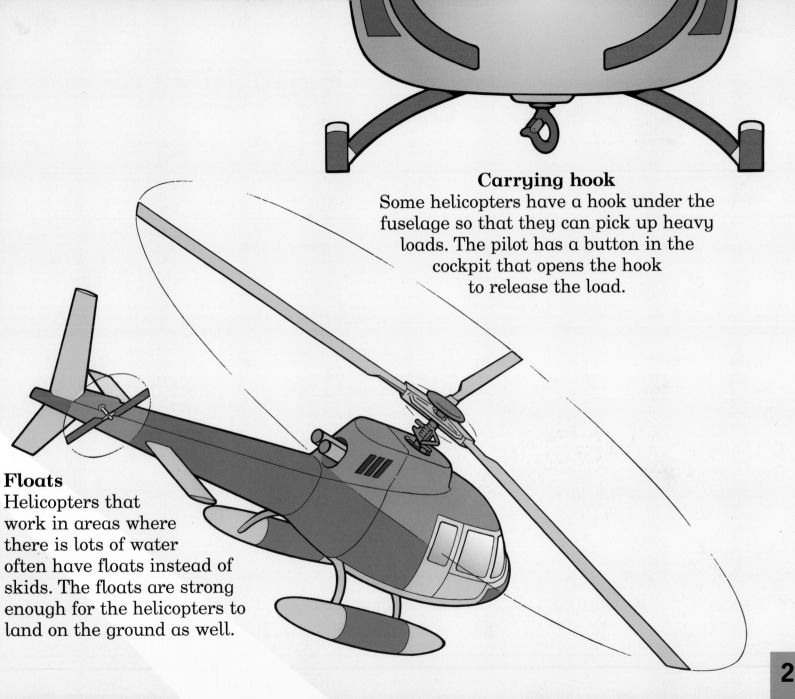

Carrying hook
Some helicopters have a hook under the fuselage so that they can pick up heavy loads. The pilot has a button in the cockpit that opens the hook to release the load.

Floats
Helicopters that work in areas where there is lots of water often have floats instead of skids. The floats are strong enough for the helicopters to land on the ground as well.

Useful Terms

cockpit The space at the front of a helicopter where the pilots sit surrounded by controls and instruments.

control column One of the controls that the pilot holds when he or she is flying the helicopter. The column controls the main rotor.

exposure suit A waterproof suit that helps to keep a person warm if he or she falls into cold water.

fin An upright piece on a helicopter's tail. It helps to keep the helicopter flying straight.

fuselage The main part of a helicopter, where the pilots and passengers sit. All the other parts are fastened to the fuselage.

galley A small kitchen in a large passenger helicopter's cabin where food and beverages are prepared.

glass fiber Thin strands of glass that are mixed with plastic to make a very strong material called glass-reinforced plastic.

hover To stay in the air without moving in any direction.

landing gear Sets of wheels under a helicopter that are used when the helicopter is moving along the ground. Smaller helicopters often have skids instead of wheels.

life jacket A jacket that inflates (fills with air) to keep a person afloat in the water. It is used when a helicopter has to make an emergency landing in water.

life raft An inflatable boat used when a helicopter has to make an emergency landing on water.

main rotor The large rotor on top of a helicopter that lifts it into the air.

pitch How much a rotor blade is tilted up. Increasing the pitch makes the leading edge (front) of the blade go up and the back of the blade go down.

rotor blade A long, thin part attached to the rotor hub at one end. Rotor blades lift the helicopter into the air as the rotor spins around.

rotor hub The piece in the center of the rotor that the rotor blades are attached to. The rotor hub is at the end of a spinning shaft.

shaft A rod that spins around, turning anything attached to it, such as a rotor or a gear wheel.

skids Metal tubes attached to the belly of a helicopter that the helicopter lands on. Smaller helicopters usually have skids, but larger ones have wheels, or landing gear, instead.

sponson A piece of a helicopter's fuselage that covers the landing gear.

stabilizer A small wing-like part that sticks out sideways from the helicopter's tail. It helps to keep the helicopter flying level.

streamlined Something that has a smooth shape that moves easily through the air.

tail The part that sticks out behind a helicopter's fuselage. The tail rotor, fin, and stabilizer are fastened to the end of the tail.

tail rotor A small rotor on the tail of most helicopters that keeps the fuselage from spinning around.

turboshaft A type of jet engine used on helicopters. It turns a shaft that makes the rotors spin.

winch A machine that pulls in or lets out a strong steel wire. Rescue helicopters have a winch for lowering a crew member who can lift people in trouble on board.

31

Index